IDEOGRAMS
IN CHINA

HENRI MICHAUX

IDEOGRAMS IN CHINA

TRANSLATED FROM THE FRENCH BY
GUSTAF SOBIN

WITH AN AFTERWORD BY
RICHARD SIEBURTH

A NEW DIRECTIONS BOOK

The original French text of *Idéogrammes en Chine* was published by Fata Morgana, Montpelier, France, in 1975.

This translation was originally published in the Fall 1984 anthology of *New Directions in Prose & Poetry 48*, and also as a limited edition by New Directions in 1984.

First published as a New Directions Paperbook (NDP929) in 2002.

Manufactured in the United States of America.
New Directions Books are printed on acid-free paper.
Published simultaneously in Canada by Penguin Books Canada Limited.

Library of Congress Cataloging-in-Publication Data:

Michaux, Henri, 1899–
[Idéogrammes en Chine. English]
Ideograms in China / Henri Michaux ; translated from the French by Gustaf Sobin ; With an afterword by Richard Sieburth.
p. cm.
ISBN 0-8112-1490-7 (pbk. : alk. Paper)
1. Chinese language—Writing—Poetry.   I. Sobin, Gustaf.   II. Title.

PQ2625.I2I3413   2002
841'.912—dc21   2001042594

New Directions Books are published for James Laughlin
by New Directions Publishing Corporation
80 Eighth Avenue, New York 10011

To Kim Chi

IDEOGRAMS
IN CHINA

*What, as apparent scribble, was once compared to the tracks of insects or the erratic footprints of birds upon sand still conveys, unchanged, perfectly legible, comprehensible, and efficacious, the Chinese language, the oldest living language in the world.

Lines going off in all directions. In every which way: commas, loops, curlicues, stress marks, seemingly at every point, at all levels: a bewildering thicket of accents.

Cracks, claw marks: the very beginnings appear to have been suddenly checked: arrested.

Without form, figure, or body, without contour, symmetry, or center, without evoking any known property whatsoever.
Without any apparent rule of simplification, unification, generalization.
Neither stripped nor refined, lacking sobriety.
Each seems, at first sight, as if scattered.*

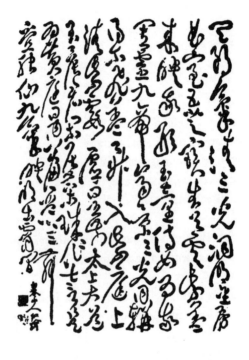

Ideograms devoid of all evocation.

Characters of an unending variety.
The page, containing them, like a lacerated void.
Lacerated by a multitude of undefined lives.

There was a time, however, when the signs still
spoke, or nearly; when, already allusive, they revealed
—rather than simple things or bodies or materials—
groups, ensembles, situations.

There was a time . . . There were others, as well.
Without making any attempt to simplify or condense,
each period obfuscating for its own particular sake,
setting things to rout, learned how to manipulate the
characters, to separate them even further—in some
new way—from their original reading.

三耆陵己南
陵洲到莫麻
天千武駝寅
戉千凸同爾
秦帛肵下武

What won out, finally, was the tendency to conceal. Reserve, prudence won out, a natural restraint, and that instinctive Chinese habit of covering one's tracks, of avoiding exposure.

What won out was the pleasure of remaining concealed. Thus the text, henceforth, covert, secret: a secret between initiates.

A long and involved secret, not readily shared, the requisite for belonging to that society within a society. That circle which, for centuries, would remain in power. That oligarchy of the subtle.

The pleasure of abstraction won out.
The brush freed the way, and paper made the going easier.

One could now readily abstract from the original reality, from the concrete and its closely related signs;

*Diminished, deformed as they are, these characters, illegible to hundreds of millions of Chinese, never entirely lost their meaning. Excluded from the inner circle of the literate, the peasantry looked upon these characters without, admittedly, understanding them, but sensing nonetheless that they came from the same place as themselves: those nimble signs, predecessors to the incurvated rooftops, to dragons and theatrical figures, to cloud drawings and landscapes with flowering branches and bamboo leaves, all of which they'd seen in pictures and knew how to appreciate.

could abstract, move swiftly with abrupt brushstrokes
that slid, unhesitating, across the paper, giving
Chinese an entirely new appearance.

Withdrawal, self-absorption won out.
Won out: the will to be mandarin.*

Gone, now, were those archaic characters that had
stirred the heart. And those signs, so palpable, that
had overwhelmed their own creators and amazed their
very first readers.

Gone, too, were the veneration and simplicity, the
earliest poetry, the tenderness that arose from the sur-
prise of the first "encounter." Gone, the still "pious"
brushstroke and the gliding ease. (Still absent, yet to
come, the intellectuals with their deft tracings: the
tracings of intellectuals . . . of scribes).

All contact cut, now, with the beginnings . . .

Innovating, at first, with prudence, but with a growing disrespect and with the joy at seeing that "it worked," that one was still being followed, understood . . .

Carried away by the seductive effrontery of their own pursuits, the inventors—those of the second period—learned how to detach the sign from its model, deforming it cautiously, at first, not yet daring to sever form from being: the umbilical, that is, of resemblance. And, in so doing, detached themselves, rejected the sacred from that earliest equation: "word-object."

Religion in writing was on the decline; the irreligion of writing had just begun.

Gone, now, were the "heartfelt" characters, so dependent upon reality. Vanished from usage, from language. They remained, however, upon the slabs of the oldest tombs, on the bronze vases dating from the earliest dynasties. Remained, too, upon divinatory bones.

Later, those early characters, sought after every-
where throughout the Middle Kingdom, meticulously
compiled and recopied, were interpreted by scholars.
An inventory, a dictionary of original signs, was
established.

Rediscovered,
and rediscovering, at the same time, the emotion
inherent in those calm, tender, tranquil first writings.

The characters, restored to their original meanings,
came back to life.

In this perspective, any written page, any surface
covered with characters turns into something crammed
and seething . . . full of lives and objects, of every-
thing to be found in the world, in the world of
China,

full of moons and hearts, full of doors
full of men who bow

who withdraw, grow angry, and make amends
full of obstacles
full of right hands, of left hands
of hands that clasp, that respond, that join forever
full of hands facing hands
of hands on guard, and others at work
full of mornings
full of doors
full of water falling, drop by drop, out of clouds
of ferryboats crossing from one side to another
full of earth embankments
of furnaces
of bows and runaways
and full, too, of disasters
and full of thieves carrying stolen goods off under
    their arms
and full of greed
and meshed armor
and full, too, of true words
and gatherings
full of children born with a caul
and holes in the earth

and of navels in the body
and full of skulls
and full of ditches
and full of migratory birds
and newborn children—and so many!
and full of metals in the depths of the earth
and full of virgin land
and fumes rising from swamps and meadows
and full of dragons
　　full of demons wandering across the open country
and full of everything that exists in the world
such as it is or assembled in some other fashion
chosen deliberately by the inventor of signs that
　　they be brought together
scenes that lend themselves to reflection
scenes of all sorts
scenes that proffer a meaning, or several meanings,
that they be submitted to the spirit
that they issue forth:
clustered that they might end in ideas
or unravel as poetry.

*Rather than calligraphy, the art of writing. With the exception of Arabic, calligraphy in other languages (when it exists) is no more than the expression of either some psychological order or, during great periods, of some ideal and often religious comportment. There is in all that a rigidity, a stiffness, a uniform stiffness that produces lines, not words, the standard corset of nobility, liturgy, of puritanical severity.

Part of that original treasure remains lost. There still exist, however, enough etymologies of an indisputable nature to permit an accomplished scholar to recognize often, running throughout, the particular origins and—in the instant of tracing the characters in their present form—to draw inspiration from the distant past.

No matter how far removed the new character is from the old, the scholar can still bring fresh life to the object by means of the word.

This is the direction he's drawn in, what his graphics aim for.

He needs no further skills, thanks to the nuance of his subtle brushstrokes.

Chinese: a language perfectly suited for calligraphy.* One that induces, provokes the inspired brushwork.

元来遺白茅
水史害退於
死之間興造
郭是後奮娃

The sign, without insistence, allows one to return to the object, to the being that, in the running text, need only be inserted into this expression quite literally expressive.

For ages the Chinese had been subject, in this field and others, to the charm of resemblance: to an immediate resemblance, at first, and then to a distant one, and finally to the composition of resembling elements.

An obstacle, as well: it had to be overcome.

Even that of the furthest resemblance. There was no returning; all similitude was to be abandoned forever.

Another destiny awaited the Chinese.

To abstract means to free oneself, to come disentangled.

*Meditation, the inner communion before a given landscape, might last twenty hours and the execution of the painting no more than twenty or thirty minutes. Here, then, is a painting that leaves room for space.

**The tiger's leap, even in religion. In Ch'an, in Zen, what stuns is the instantaneity of the illumination.

The destiny that awaited Chinese writing was utter weightlessness.

The characters that evolved were better suited than their archaic predecessors in terms of speed, agility, deftness of gesture. A certain kind of Chinese landscape painting demands speed, can only be executed with the same sudden release as the paw of a springing tiger. (For which one must first be concentrated, self-contained and, at the same time, relaxed).*

The calligrapher, likewise, must first be plunged in meditation, be charged with energy in order to release: to discharge that very energy. And all at once.**

The necessary knowledge—the "four treasures" of the writer's chamber (brush, paper, ink, and inkstone)—is extensive, complex. But then . . .

The hand should be empty, should in no way hinder what's flowing into it. Should be ready for the least sensation as well as the most violent. A bearer of influx, of effluvia.

*Deep ripples or shallow ones, ripples of water running or falling in waterfalls to re-emerge, bubbling, onto the surface. Certain painters are famous for their water ripples, as the venerable Wang Wei for having discovered the ripple "of the rain and snow."

. . . In a certain way similar to water, to both its lightest and most vigorous properties, its least apparent, such as ripples,* which have always been a subject of study in China.

Even before the advent of Buddhism, water—the image itself of detachment, bound to nothing and ready, at every instant, to continue its course—spoke to the very heart of the Chinese people. Water, the absence of form.

Yi Tin, Yi Yang, tche wei Tao
Alternately Yin, alternately Yang
This is the way; this, the tao.

The way traced by writing.

To be a calligrapher, as one might be a landscape painter. Even better, for in China a calligrapher is considered the salt of the earth.

In this particular calligraphy—this art of the temporal, expressing as it does trajectory, passage—its most admirable quality (even more than its harmony or vivacity) is its spontaneity. This spontaneity runs, sometimes, to the point of shattering.

No longer to imitate, but signify nature. By strokes, darts, dashes.

Ascesis of the immediate, of the lightning bolt.

The sign in Chinese, today, which is no longer in any way mimetic, has the grace of its own impatience. It has drawn from nature its flight, its diversity, its inimitable way of knowing how to bend, rebound, redress itself.

Like nature, the Chinese language does not draw any conclusions of its own, but lets itself be read.

Its meager syntax leaves room for guesswork, for creativity, leaves space for poetry. Out of the multiple issues the idea.

Characters open onto several directions at once.

Point of pure equilibrium.

Every language is a parallel universe. And none more lovely than Chinese.

Calligraphy enhances it, for it completes the poem, is the expression that gives the poem its validity and, at the same time, vouches for the poet.

An exact balance between opposites, the art of the calligrapher (both in its separate steps and overall procedures) consists in revealing himself to the world. Like a Chinese actor entering on stage and giving his name and birthplace, then relating what has happened and what he is about to do, the calligrapher envelopes himself in his own motivations, furnishes his own justifications. It is apparent, in calligraphy, by the way one handles signs whether one is truly lettered, is truly worthy of the art. By this criterion alone, one is —or is not—justified.

Calligraphy in its role as mediator between communion and abeyance.

What might have happened if some Western language had had even a fraction of the calligraphic possibilities as Chinese? The baroque that would have ensued, along with the happenstance discoveries of individualists, all the rarities and peculiarities, the eccentricities of every possible kind.

Chinese was equal to all of this. Everywhere it offers up new possibilities; its every character serves as a fresh temptation.

If one takes, from various authors, a specific character, one that is easily recognizable, attractive, and charged with sense, and detaches it from both text and context, the word "heart" for example, no matter how far removed the brushstrokes might be from anything that might resemble a heart, the heart will, nonetheless, by its tracing, take on—with each calligrapher—a particular life of its own. One can readily see, among various calligraphers, how each time it is the same, and each time entirely different. One heart is generous, and another high-spirited. One heart would deceive while yet another would

夫靈蹤威

則舉宗廙尋

welcome: be good to live with. There is a heart at
deep peace with itself, and a heart that is warm,
well-disposed. Or the heart unruffled, that nothing
troubles, that saves its own skin every time. Or one
that is fickle, that settles nowhere, or another that is
fearsome, and still another, submissive. There is a
heart, too, that—at the drop of a hat—would take
flight. Or the meddlesome heart, or the heart expect-
ant, or venturous, or dry, or placid, or—to the
contrary—the dauntless heart that nothing can stop.
Or the entirely attentive, the perfect heart that even
on a fibrous sheet of rice paper can last centuries and
still manage to astonish.

To every calligrapher, the life, the proprietorship of
the heart is offered. But not for the sake of origi-
nality, unless it be muted, unless he himself be
scarcely suggested.

It is considered base, vulgar to behave ostentatiously.

Only the "exact placement," the "just proportion"
matter.

*Free calligraphy.
In Japan, all kinds of freedom have been taken and new pleasures derived from excessive practices in calligraphy. This freedom might, someday—who knows?—swarm across all of Chinese Asia.

And the perfect page is the one that "seems traced at a single go."

China, righteous and mindful as it was of harmony, would have scarcely appreciated the buffoon.

Writing must possess an invigorating quality. For writing is a way of life.

A perfect, an exemplary balance must be maintained. Even among those fanatics, commonly called "the madmen of calligraphy," who went without eating, drinking, and sleeping, and who had lost all sense of measure in their lives, the very instant they picked up their brushes, they would trace characters entirely free of any imbalance; characters, to the contrary, filled with a new and masterful equilibrium.
The highest order is always dynamic.

And so Chinese writing was saved from both the rigid and the baroque,* the two traps of calligraphy.

China, land where one meditated upon the tracings of a calligrapher as, in other countries, one would meditate upon a mantra, or upon substance, essence, or fundamental principles.

Calligraphy around which—quite simply—one might abide as next to a tree, or a rock, or a source.

SIGNS IN ACTION:
MICHAUX / POUND

BY RICHARD SIEBURTH

In his obituary memoir of Ezra Pound, Guy Davenport notes that during his final years in Venice *il miglior fabbro*, having abandoned his Cantos as a colossal botch, having edged further and further into silence, was nevertheless contemplating a translation of Henri Michaux's *Idéogrammes en Chine*. Pound's health was failing, as was his confidence in the word, and apparently after a few false starts the project was set aside. It was left to a younger American poet, Gustaf Sobin, to complete the task—with the result that Michaux's *Ideograms in China* was finally made available to English-speaking readers in 1984, published in a limited edition of 150 copies by New Directions as a latterday complement to Ernest Fenollosa's classic study, *The Chinese Written Character as a Medium for Poetry*.[1]

Literary history is of course filled with such failed encounters—dialogues abandoned en route, aborted conversations—but it seems to me that the juncture of Pound and Michaux, however tenuous, however mute it might have been, is especially resonant, for here was Pound at the dusk of his career circling back to beginnings, returning once again to the ideograms he had first learned to haruspicate in 1913 with the aid of Fenollosa's manuscript on the Chinese character, and returning, moreover in the company of a French poet whose own graphic and literary work had since the late 20s been engaging the gist and gesture of Chinese ideogram with an intensity and an originality matched by few other artists of the 20th century.

A translation of a French poet's meditations on Chinese calligraphy—the configuration is typically Poundian (think of the first Canto, a translation into Anglo-Saxonized English of a Renaissance Latin version of Homer). And if Michaux's French prose poetry acts as a mediator in this transaction between East and West, Chinese and English, this too is another memory of beginnings, a trace of the China Pound first discovered in French guise—whether it be via Pauthier's versions of Confucius or via Judith Gautier's *Livre de jade* whose delicate *chinoiseries* Pound would extend into the haiku-like condensations of the Imagist lyric or the poems of *Cathay* (1915). Pound's China, a realm where Mencius speaks to Mussolini and Confucius converses with the Adams dynasty in an idiom that blends the civic apothegms of the Encyclopedists with the hermetic evanescence of a Mallarmé, is an imaginary kingdom as quirky as any of those to be found in Michaux's *Voyage en Grande Garabagne*. I take Pound's late, silent dialogue with Michaux's *Idéogrammes en Chine* as a final, failed gesture toward this imaginary China—a last visit to the Empire of Signs (to use Barthes' term) or (if one prefers Genette) a belated *voyage en Cratylie*.

Blanchot observes in an essay on Michaux and Borges that one of the tasks of criticism is to render all comparison impossible.[2] I would therefore like to proceed by simply juxtaposing, rather than explicitly comparing, Pound's and Michaux's encounters with the Chinese character, in the hope that such a juxtaposition might tell us something about larger issues involving modernism, Cratylism, and the poetics of the sign. I use the term juxtaposition deliberately because it is fundamental to what Pound calls the "ideogrammic method," a method that underlies both the formal and didactic design of the *Cantos*.

Pound called his poetics "ideogrammic" because he followed the sinologist Fenollosa in believing (rightly or wrongly) that the sense of individual Chinese characters was visibly generated by the juxtaposition of their graphic (or graphemic) components. Fenollosa writes, for example:

> *The ideograph "to speak" is a mouth with two words and a flame coming out of it. The sign meaning "to grow up with difficulty" is grass with a twisted root. . . . In this process of compounding, two things added together do not produce a third thing but suggest some fundamental relation between them. For example, the ideograph for a "messmate" is a man and a fire. (pp. 8–9)*

The key term here is *relation,* for as Fenollosa writes elsewhere in this same essay (predicting the structuralists): "Relations are more real and more important than the things they relate" (p. 22). Which Pound footnotes: "Compare Aristotle's Poetics: 'Swift perception of relations, hallmark of genius.' "

Such "swift perception of relations," associated by Aristotle with the intuition of metaphor, is what a poem like Pound's 1913 "In a Station of the Metro" is out to record and instigate. The original printing emphasized the intervals that punctuate the poem, each semantic or rhythmic cluster functioning as a discrete, autonomous character, three characters to each line:

> *The apparition   of these faces   in a crowd:*
> *Petals   on a wet, black   bough*

This technique of ideogrammic juxtaposition, still relatively simple and straightforward in Pound's "Metro" haiku, is applied at a number of levels in the *Cantos.* Only the scale of the units thus placed in relation changes, ranging from single words or tag phrases to complete lines or blocks of lines to entire Cantos or sequences of Cantos. Rather than explicitly articulating the syntactical (or narrative) connectives between the items thus juxtaposed, rather than subordinating one to another (hypotaxis), Pound instead situates his material side by side on the same flat surface as equivalent units of design (parataxis). Pound's paratactic disposition of seemingly unrelated particulars has of course been frequently compared to modernist practices of collage or assemblage, but it's worth emphasizing that he conceived of his poetic method not only in the context of avant-garde experiment, but as a recovery of something profoundly traditional or archaic—after all, both the compound graphic and semantic structure of the Chinese character and the perfected parataxis of classical Chinese poetry seemed proof enough that other languages, other grammars of art were indeed possible.[3] Sergei Eisenstein, for one, came to similar conclusions about the unexplored linguistic possibilities of cinematic montage after studying Chinese ideograms, as witnessed by the title of his 1929 essay, "The Cinematographic Principle and the Ideograph," a text roughly contemporary with Michaux's first graphic experiments with those imaginary alphabets or rebuses he would later term "ideogram compositions" or "cinematic drawings."[4]

Pound, Eisenstein, Michaux—a critical ideogram comprised of three names working in three different media, here assembled merely to indicate the extent to which the Chinese character, from the time of Leibniz all the way up to Sollers, has tended to speak primarily to Western *eyes* (and this despite the fact that 90% of Chinese characters are in fact *phonetic* compounds). The Imagist Pound was delighted to find in Chinese a language of signs so pictorially suggestive that his friend the French sculptor Gaudier-Brzeska could pick up a Chinese dictionary and effortlessly read the forms of many radicals at sight.

Pound's mentor Fenollosa, steeped as he was in the American Transcendentalist tradition, encouraged his conviction that Chinese was a perfect natural language since it represented not sounds, but rather the "visible hieroglyphics" of Nature itself. Take, for example, Fenollosa's gloss on the Chinese sentence "Man sees horse."

> But Chinese notation is something much more than arbitrary symbols. It is based upon a vivid shorthand picture of the operations of nature. In the algebraic figure and in the spoken word there is no natural connection between thing and sign: all depends on sheer convention. But the Chinese method follows natural suggestion. First stands the man on his two legs. Second, his eye moves through space; a bold figure represented by running legs under an eye. . . . Third stands the horse on his four legs. . . . Legs belong to all three characters; they are alive. The group holds something of the quality of a continuous moving picture. (pp. 8–9)

If one wanted to translate Fenollosa's analysis into Jakobsonian terms, one could say that according to this account, the poetic function of Chinese is foregrounded by the visual form of the signifier itself; one can actually *see* how the axis of selection (the legs the three characters have in common) has been projected onto the axis of combination. For Fenollosa the Chinese character is intrinsically poetic in another sense as well, for it bears "its metaphor on its face" (p. 25): the sign for sun glows like a sun, the sign for tree grows like a tree, and when you combine the two, entangling the sun radical in the branches of the tree, you have represented East. One need only leaf through Genette's *Mimologiques* to recognize Fenollosa's mirage of a non-arbitrary, fully motivated language as a familiar avatar of Cratylism. Indeed, commenting on Claudel's 1898 "Religion du signe" (included in *Connaissance de l'Est*) and his later *Idéogrammes occidentaux* (1926), Genette observes that the Chinese logogram has tended to play the same role in 20th-century Cratylism that the Egyptian hieroglyph played in the 19th.[5]

Fenollosa's picture theory of Chinese, however, does not merely rest on the assumption of a one-to-one correspondence between the sign and what it represents; rather, he is more concerned with *groups* or *systems* of signs, with signs in relation, in movement, in process.[6] Hence the emphasis on Chinese as a cinematic "moving picture," on Chinese word order as a "transference of power" from agent to object, and hence the insistence that Chinese is composed not of nouns, but of verbs:

> *A true noun, an isolated thing, does not exist in nature. Things are only the terminal points, or rather the meeting points, of actions, cross-sections cut through actions, snapshots. Neither can a pure verb, an abstract motion, be possible in nature. The eye sees noun and verb as one: things in motion, motion in things, and so the Chinese conception tends to represent them. (p. 10)*

"Things in motion, motion in things"—the mimology proposed here is based less (to use Peirce's terminology) on the iconic resemblance between the sign and what it represents than on an indexical relation of causality or contiguity between the two. Indeed, if Fenollosa or Pound consider Chinese the ideal medium for poetry, it is because its characters actually mime or respond to the very processes of Nature in a language whose signs are visibly patterned by the primal energies of the elements (much as, in Peirce's example of the indexical sign, the wind causes the weathervane to register its direction). Answering to a *natura naturans,* a nature in process, in the making, Chinese writing thus becomes a *scriptura scribens,* a writing in and of process. Fenollosa's post-Romantic insistence on *energeia* over *ergon* ("the verb must be the primary fact of nature," "The cherry tree is all that it does") not only had a great deal to do with Pound's own drift from estheticism into activist politics (a poet is all that he does, however grievously he might err in the process), but it also served to shape his conception of the *Cantos* as a kind of gigantic Action Poem—not an autonomous textual artifact, not a noun, but a verb, an ongoing enactment of individual and collective process, a performative experiment open to whatever might at the moment be at hand, including its own incompletion or eventual ruin.

I have deliberately borrowed the notion of an Action Poem from the vocabulary of modern art history (it was Harold Rosenberg who was the first to speak of Action Painting)[7] because it provides an obvious bridge into Michaux—poet, painter, actor, in short, inscriber of actions or agons on canvas or page, performer of dramatic events that invite reading as signs, traces of movement, vestiges of gesture. Scholars of Michaux concur in emphasizing the centrality of *le geste* to his entire work—whether it be the onomatopoetic vocal gesticulations of Michaux's "nonsense" verse or the calligraphic pantomime that is a trademark of his drawings.[8] Michaux describes as follows the process recorded in *Mouvements,* a series of some 1200 sheets of ideogrammic signs enacted in *encre de Chine* over the course of 1950–51: "It involved gestures, interiors, for which we have no limbs at our disposal but only the desire of limbs, tensions, élans, all made up of living cords, never thick, never swollen with flesh or enclosed in skin."[9] Gestures incarnating, dramatizing something beyond or before the body, gestures realizing themselves in or as signs, the sheer generation or proliferation of which allows Michaux to leave words behind:

> *It's precisely because I managed to liberate myself from words,*
> *these sticky hangers-on, that the drawings are so slender and*
> *almost joyous, that their movements were so easy for me to*
> *execute, despite their occasional exasperations. I see in them a*
> *new language, turning its back on the verbal, a liberator . . .*
> *an unexpected, soothing mode of writing in which one would*
> *finally be able to express oneself far from words, far from other*
> *people's words.*[10]

To which one might juxtapose Julia Kristeva's essay on gesture in *Semiotikē* which addresses gestuality as an instance of sheer production, sheer expenditure, in other words, as a semiotic practice that puts into question not only the conventional communicative function of verbal language, but more crucially the phonocentric priority generally accorded to voice by Western linguistics and metaphysics.[11] Kristeva bases much of her notion of gesture on Tchang Tcheng-Ming's *L'Ecriture chinoise et le geste humain* (1937), the very same book, it turns out, that inspired Claudel's "La figure, le mouvement et le geste dans l'ecriture en Chine et en Occident."[12] Although Kristeva wants to consider gesture not in terms of representation or expression, but rather as a kind of anaphora or index (in the Husserlian sense of *Anzeichen*), her vocabulary oddly echoes Fenollosa's: "Before and behind *voice* and *writing* there is anaphora: the gesture that *indicates,* that institutes *relations* and eliminates entities. The semiotic system of the Dogon [Kristeva's semiotopia now migrates from China to Africa] which in the end seems to be more a scriptural semantic system than a verbal one, is thus based on *indication*: for them, to learn to speak is to learn to indicate by tracing."[13]

– 46 –

This revisionary Derridean myth of origins, which stages the anteriority of *écriture* (writing, marking, tracing, drawing) to speech, brings us to Michaux's own *Fable des origines,* to quote the title of one of his earliest books (1923). In his semiautobiographical *Emergences-Résurgences* (1972), he tells the origin story of his own career as a writer-painter. In the beginning was the line, the trace, the traversal and division of space:

> *One day, later in life, I too feel the impulse to draw, to participate in the world by lines. One line, rather than many lines. And so I begin, allowing myself to be led by a single line, giving it free rein without so much as lifting pencil from paper— until, having wandered restlessly in this restricted space, it inevitably comes to a stop.*[14]

This is line as sheer process, having no other motive than its own exploratory traversal of the field of the page. This nomadic, somnambulistic line, a kind of seismographic indicator of the aleatory psychic and physical vectors that have converged on the page, is Michaux's own version of surrealistic automatic writing. But having given himself over to line, to pure *parcours* or *trajet,* Michaux soon finds himself confronting signs: pages emerge covered with imaginary alphabets (which he calls "pictographs" or "ideographs"), their squiggles and strokes arranged into furrows of writing.

Here is Michaux's restrospective account of these *Alphabets* or *Narrations* that he drew/wrote in 1927:

> *Later, the signs, certain signs. Signs speak to me. I would gladly draw them, but a sign is also a stop sign. And at this juncture there is still something I desire above all else. A continuum. A murmur without end, like life itself, the thing that keeps us going. . . . I want my markings ("mes tracés") to be*

the very phrasing ("le phrasé") of life, but supple, deformable, sinuous.[15]

On the one hand, Michaux's move from the single unbroken line into a series of signs embodies an attempt to discover a kind of language or semiotic system that goes beyond (or before) the conventionalized marks of writing or pictorial representation—a series of signifiers without signifieds (or rather, that would simply signify the desire to write, draw, inscribe, sign), a purely private alphabet that would free him from having to speak (or draw) like anybody else, a succession of signs that one might term *idio*grams (somewhat on the order of the private nonsense language he was experimenting with during this same period in the poems of *Qui je fus*). On the other hand, Michaux's discovery of signs is, as he notes, also an encounter with a certain kind of blockage or stoppage, for as the continuous line breaks up into a sequence or grouping of signs, an impetus is lost, a fixity sets in, the flow of traffic now halted by stop signs—"un signe, c'est aussi un signal d'arrêt."

Such stasis or arrest of course goes directly counter to Michaux's desire to embody a continuum, a *durée,* an unbroken murmur of motion—and the fact that he titles these imaginary alphabets or pictograms *Narrations* indicates just how far this aesthetic of continuity lies from Pound's paratactic ideograms which aim instead at pulverizing the syntax of narrative, at erasing transitions, at opening up intervals and breaches by a constructivist technique of collage or jumpcut montage that serves to isolate the signs thus juxtaposed. Michaux, by contrast, wants to surmount such segmentation, to eliminate the problematic space *in between* by the sheer rapidity of his traversal through it. His mescaline writings and drawings of the 50s, for example, register a state of flux where there is virtually no intervening vacuum between images or marks, but rather a plenum of uninterrupted pulsations and oscillations.[16] Similarly, if Michaux's poetry favors prose lineation over lines of verse (and a prose, moreover, that is often narrative in thrust), it is largely because he is after a fluidity or kinesis that will somehow enact the ongoing pulse or tempo of *l'élan vital*.

Michaux's early ideogrammic drawings, he tells us in *Emergences-Résurgences*, led to an impasse or *échec* that caused him to abandon painting altogether for a number of years. It was only in the course of his travels to the Far East in 1930–31 that he suddenly recognized what he had been looking for in his earlier explorations of lines and signs:

> But it is Chinese painting that enters into me in depth, converts me. As soon as I see it, I become a complete adept of the world of signs and lines. Distances preferred to proximities, the poetry of incompletion preferred to eyewitness accounts, to copies. Markings launched into the air, fluttering as if caught by the motion of a sudden inspiration, and not prosaically, laboriously, exhaustively traced. . . . this is what spoke to me, what seized me, what carried me away. This time, the cause of painting had been won.[17]

In *A Barbarian in Asia*, Michaux's 1933 travelogue of this same journey, he similarly underscores the importance of this semiotic encounter with the exotic, for in China he discovered a tradition of painting, writing, and theater that was at once concrete and abstract, material and immaterial, stable and fluid—a tradition, in short, grounded not in mimesis, not in copying, but rather in the art of *signification*:

> The Chinese have a talent for reducing being to signified being (something like the talent for algebra or math). If a battle is to take place, they do not serve up a battle, they do not simulate

it. They signify it. This is the only thing that interests them,
the actual battle would strike them as vulgar.[18]

Or as Michaux later puts it in *Ideograms in China*: "No longer imitate nature. Signify it. By marks ("traits"), by élans." The French word *trait*, as Barthes observes, is a term shared both by the graphic arts and by linguistics.[19] It suggests a kind of diacritical marking that is fundamental to the Chinese conception of *wen*, a character that signifies a conglomeration of marks, whether these be the veins of stones or of wood, the strokes that connect stars into constellations, the tracks of animals on the ground, or finally, the art of writing, of literature, and of social courtesy.[20]

Michaux's 1931 visit to the Empire of Signs, according to his own account, verified his vocation as an adept of *wen*, as an adventurer in that semiotic no-man's-land that exists somewhere between (or perhaps before) visual and verbal language. An entire strand of Michaux's graphic work shows his drawing or painting constantly moving toward the territory of writing. His early *Alphabets* or *Narrations* of 1927 will resurface in the rebuses of *Epreuves, Exorcismes* (1945), the ideogrammic élans of *Mouvements* (1951), the serial gouache bestiaries of 1952, the India and sepia ink canvases of 1961–62, the gouache calligrams of 1965–66, or the anthropomorphic acrylics and aquarelles of the 70s. But if the graphic so often tends toward the graphemic in Michaux, the reverse is also true, perhaps nowhere more so than in the 1956 mescaline drawings of *Misérable Miracle* in which the horizontal lettering of actual words on the page gradually disintegrates into a series of unintelligible vertical or transversal strokes that resemble the gibberish penmanship of a Saul Steinberg or the unreadable tags of a subway graffiti artist.

Michaux's explorations of the process whereby drawing or painting translate into writing and vice versa (to which one should also add his many books in which the illustrative relation of text to image is virtually reversible) prepare his 1971 return to China in *Idéogrammes en Chine,* a late, mellow meditation on his own career in and amongst signs, an *ars poetica* that reads like an autumnal episode in the adventures of Monsieur Plume. *Ideograms in China* was initially written as an introduction to Léon Tchang's *La Calligraphie chinoise.* The text therefore presents itself in the form of a commentary or, to quote the title of Michaux's book on Magritte, *En rêvant à partir de peintures enigmatiques* (1964), as a revery inspired by the samples of Chinese calligraphy that intersperse his French text and provide the themes on which his commentary will play its variations. Just as Michaux takes Magritte's paintings and turns them into stories, so *Ideograms* links its visual pretexts into a chronicle evoking the genealogy and evolution of Chinese writing. Its overall plot may be summarized as follows: 1) writing at its origin, 2) the loss of origin, 3) the recovery of origin via etymology, 4) writing-as-representation moving toward writing-as-signification, and 5) the return, via abstraction, to Nature and origins. As this rough outline might make clear, Michaux's essay on the ideogram enacts a kind of dialectical oscillation between origin and derivation, absence and presence, representation and signification, a movement that leads in the end to an equilibrium or "just balance of opposites" embodied by calligraphy in its role as a "mediator" between "communication and suspension."

As in the Fenollosa-Pound essay on the Chinese character, a Cratylistic nostalgia haunts Michaux's meditations on calligraphy. After a brief introductory section that registers the inevitable bewilderment of the Western eye upon first encountering a page of Chinese calligraphy ("Lines going off in all directions. In every which way: commas, loops, curlicues, stress marks, seemingly at every point, at all levels: a bewildering thicket of accents"), Michaux passes beyond this stage of origi-

gion of writing had just begun." Sacred gives way to secular scripture.

But in this world of the Fall, where writing now functions as an agent of exclusion and concealment, there is nonetheless hope of redemption: as scholars piously regather the ancient characters into indexes (circa 120 A.D.), a first etymological dictionary (the *Shuo-wen*) is born, restoring words to their origins, resurrecting the characters from their tombs of abstraction. At this etymological juncture Michaux's text suddenly soars into a Whitmanesque (or Borgesian) catalogue of this rediscovered plentitude—an inventory of the wealth of a world again filled with people, things, events, signs:

> *full of moons, and hearts, full of doors*
> *full of men who bow*
> *who withdraw, grow angry, and make amends*
> *full of obstacles*
> *full of right hands, of left hands*
> *of hands that clasp, that respond, that join forever*
> *full of hands facing hands*
> *of hands on guard, and others at work*
> *full of mornings*
> *full of doors*

These anaphoras continue for two pages, a familiar variant on one of Michaux's favorite modes—the abecedarium, the bestiary, the taxonomy, the serial proliferation of signs. This profusion is made possible by an etymological perspective that re-situates (or remotivates) the sign in relation to its source—as Fenollosa remarked, poets proceed by "feeling back along the ancient lines of advance," a process particularly evident in Michaux's own ideogrammic drawings and paintings which are in a sense etymologies of gesture, enactments of their own origin, mimings of the moment at which signs, not yet fully bearers of sense, begin to *come into being.*

This explains, I think, why Michaux's allegorical history of the ideogram should now move from etymology into the next stage, the development of calligraphy—the sign in (or as) action. The increasingly stylized strokes of the calligrapher represent for Michaux a further (and higher) retreat from iconicity, from resemblance:

> *For ages the Chinese had been subject, in this field and others, to the charm of resemblance: to an immediate resemblance, at first, and then to a distant one, and finally to the composition of resembling elements.*
>
> *An obstacle, as well: it had to be overcome.*
>
> *Even that of the furthest resemblance. There was no returning; all similitude was to be abandoned forever.*
>
> *Another destiny awaited the Chinese.*
>
> *To abstract means to free oneself, to come disentangled.*

Abstraction, associated earlier with secrecy and concealment and serving the hegemony of a scribal elite, now re-emerges as a religious ascesis or gnosis. Ritualized into the art of calligraphy, this action writing/painting completely dematerializes the world into a condition of pure speed, pure flight, pure mind: "The destiny that awaited Chinese writing was utter weightlessness." But if calligraphy enables the material body of the sign to be transfigured into pure spirit, the very activity of this *scriptura scribens* nonetheless plunges us back (by a kind of dialectical reversal) into the immanent energies of a *natura naturans*. Freed from imitating nature, signs may now signify it, respond to it, participate in its *wen*:

> *No longer to imitate, but to signify nature. By strokes, darts, dashes.*

Ascesis of the immediate, of the lightning bolt.

The sign in Chinese, today, which is no longer in any way mimetic, has the grace of its own impatience. It has drawn from nature its flight, its diversity, its inimitable way of knowing how to bend, rebound, redress itself.

Like nature, the Chinese language does not draw any conclusions of its own, but lets itself be read . . .

Characters open onto several directions at once.

Point of pure equilibrium . . .

Calligraphy in its role as mediator between communion and abeyance . . .

Calligraphy around which—quite simply—one might abide as next to a tree, or a rock, or a source.

At the end of this long detour through China, Michaux thus rediscovers a modernist version of the ancient dream of Cratylus, a semiotopia in which all his works, all his gestures, all his *tracés* will bespeak *le phrasé* of natural process. The agons of his earlier work now give way to the late serenity of *Jours de silence* (1978), the sign pulsing at the heart of stillness:

Certitude vibrante
sa touche si fine, qui fait signe
cime et abîme sur la même ligne

Vibrant certainty
its touch so fine, making a sign
peak, abyss on the same line.

NOTES

1 Michaux's *Idéogrammes en Chine* was first printed as a preface to Leon Tchang Long Yen's *La Calligraphie chinoise* (Paris: Club français du Livre, 1971) and then published separately by Fata Morgana in 1975. All subsequent page references to Ernest Fenollosa, *The Chinese Written Character as a Medium for Poetry*, Ezra Pound ed., (San Francisco: City Lights, n.d.) will be included in the body of the text.

2 Maurice Blanchot, "L'infini et l'infini," in *Henri Michaux*, Raymond Bellour, ed. (Paris: Ed. de l'Herne, 1966), p. 80.

3 For a fuller treatment of Pound's "ideogrammic method" and its relation to the American tradition of Williams, Olson, Duncan, Ginsberg, and Snyder, see Laszlo Géfin, *Ideogram: History of a Poetic Method* (Austin: U. of Texas, 1982). See also Haroldo de Campos, "Poetic Function and Ideogram/The Sinological Argument," *Journal of Hispanic Philology*, vol. VI, no. 17–18 (1981), pp. 9–39. Further perspectives are provided by Zhaoming Qian, *Orientalism and Modernism: The Legacy of China in Pound and Williams* (Durham: Duke U., 1995) and Robert Kern, *Orientalism, Modernism, and the American Poem* (Cambridge: Cambridge U., 1996).

4 See Hugh Kenner, *The Pound Era* (Berkeley: U. of California, 1971), p. 162.

5 Gérard Genette, *Mimologics*, trans. Thaïs E. Morgan (Lincoln: U. of Nebraska, 1995), p. 267.

6 It should be pointed out that the mimological mirage of the Chinese ideogram as a "picture" of natural process is perhaps less crucial to

Pound's actual handling of poetic language in his *Cantos* than it is to his economic theory, whose major obsession turns on the issue of the accurate "monetary representation" or the faithful "money picture" of available goods. Not the least of the *Cantos'* many paradoxes lies in the fact that while the poem's central concerns involve the fate of political or economic *representation* in the modern world, its actual linguistic texture is best described not in terms of *mimesis* but rather as a product of *semiosis*, signs interpreting other signs. Michaux's meditations on the Chinese character are informed by a similar oscillation between the notion of *representation* on the one hand, and that of *signification* on the other.

7   Harold Rosenberg, *The Tradition of the New* (New York: Horizon Press, 1959).

8   See, for example, Michel Beaujour "Sens et Nonsense" in the Cahier L'Herne devoted to Michaux, pp. 133–142, and Jean Starobinski, "Le Monde physionomique," in *Henri Michaux* (Paris: Centre Georges Pompidou, 1974), pp. 65–67.

9   *Henri Michaux,* ibid., p. 69. My translation.

10   Ibid., p. 71.

11   Julia Kristeva, "Le geste, pratique ou communication?" in *Semiotikē* (Paris: Seuil, 1969), pp. 29–51.

12   Jean-Claude Coquet, "La lettre et les idéogrammes occidentaux," *Poétique* 11 (1972), p. 401.

13   Kristeva, p. 35.

14   *Emergences-Resurgences,* trans. Richard Sieburth (Milan: Skira, 2000), p. 10.

15   Ibid., p. 11.

16   See Malcolm Bowie, *Henri Michaux* (Oxford: Oxford U. Press, 1973), pp. 161–163.

17   *Emergences-Resurgences,* p. 12.

18   *Un Barbare en Asie* (Paris: Gallimard, 1933), pp. 156–157. It might be noted in passing that this book was translated into English for New Directions in 1949 by Shakespeare and Company's Sylvia Beach, who also induced Joyce biographer Richard Ellmann to translate Michaux's *Selected Writings* (New Directions, 1968).

19   Roland Barthes, *Empire of Signs*, trans. Richard Howard (New York: Hill and Wang, 1982), p. 3.

20   On *wen*, see François Cheng, *Chinese Poetic Writing*, trans. Donald Riggs and Jerome Seaton (Bloomington: Indiana U., 1982), p. 213, and Jacques Derrida, *Of Grammatology*, trans. Gayatri Chakravorty Spivak (Baltimore: Johns Hopkins, 1976), pp. 91–92 (where Pound and Fenollosa are also mentioned).